FANTASTICALLY FUNNY FOOTBALL JOKE BOOK

Sch

FANTASTICALLY FUNNY FOOTBALL
JOKE BOOK

DAVE BROMAGE, RHODRI CROOKS
AND KAY WOODWARD
ILLUSTRATED BY JOHN KELLY

PUFFIN

PUFFIN BOOKS

Published by the Penguin Group
Penguin Books Ltd, 80 Strand, London WC2R 0RL, England
Penguin Group (USA) Inc., 375 Hudson Street, New York, New York 10014, USA
Penguin Group (Canada), 90 Eglinton Avenue East, Suite 700, Toronto, Ontario, Canada M4P 2Y3
(a division of Pearson Penguin Canada Inc.)
Penguin Ireland, 25 St Stephen's Green, Dublin 2, Ireland (a division of Penguin Books Ltd)
Penguin Group (Australia), 250 Camberwell Road, Camberwell, Victoria 3124, Australia
(a division of Pearson Australia Group Pty Ltd)
Penguin Books India Pvt Ltd, 11 Community Centre, Panchsheel Park, New Delhi – 110 017, India
Penguin Group (NZ), cnr Airborne and Rosedale Roads, Albany, Auckland 1310, New Zealand
(a division of Pearson New Zealand Ltd)
Penguin Books (South Africa) (Pty) Ltd, 24 Sturdee Avenue, Rosebank, Johannesburg 2196, South Africa

Penguin Books Ltd, Registered Offices: 80 Strand, London WC2R 0RL, England

www.penguin.com

First published 2006
1

Text copyright © Puffin Books, 2006
Illustrations copyright © John Kelly, 2006
All rights reserved

British Library Cataloguing in Publication Data
A CIP catalogue record for this book is available from the British Library

ISBN-13: 978–0–141–32115–6
ISBN-10: 0–141–32115–6

CONTENTS

THE WACKY WORLD CUP

THESE WACKY WORLD CUP JOKES ARE SURE-FIRE WINNERS!

⚽ Why did the winning team spin their trophy round and round?

🏆 It was the Whirled Cup.

⚽ Which English footballer is always in debt?

🏆 Michael Owing.

⚽ How does Sven-Göran Eriksson drive to work?

🏆 In a 4x4x2.

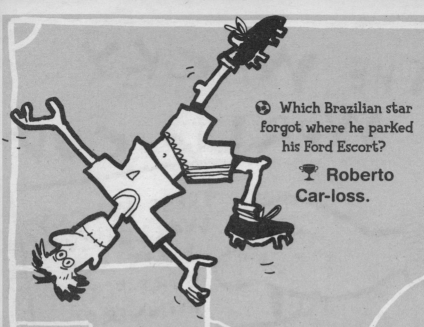

⚽ Which Brazilian star forgot where he parked his Ford Escort?

🏆 Roberto Car-loss.

⚽ Victoria Beckham comes back from the shops and finds the England captain jumping up and down in excitement.
'Forty-three days, forty-three days!' he shouts.
'I've finished this jigsaw in only forty-three days!'
'What's so good about that?' asks Victoria.
'Well,' says David, 'it says three to six years on the box!'

⚽ What comes from Central America, has 120,000 hands and whooshes around a football stadium?

🏆 A Mexican wave.

⚽ Why did Wayne Rooney take jam to the England training session?

🏆 He heard Sven was going to give him a free role.

PREPOSTEROUS PLAYERS

WITH TEAM-MATES LIKE THESE, WHO NEEDS AN OPPOSITION?

⚽ Why did the striker play in his living room?

🏆 It was a home game.

⚽ Why did the footballers suddenly start to trip over?

🏆 They were playing injury time.

⚽ A footballer turns up for a game with both his ears bandaged up. 'What happened to your ears?' asks his manager.

The footballer replies, 'Yesterday I was ironing my shirt when the phone rang. I accidentally answered the iron.'
'That explains one ear, but what happened to the other one?' asks the manager.
'Well, then I had to call the doctor!'

⚽ Did you hear about the striker who tricked the defender and then passed out?

🏆 He feinted.

⚽ Why do footballers carry handkerchiefs?

🏆 They're always dribbling.

How did the vegetarian footballer get injured?

He pulled a cheese-string.

What type of houses do footballers live in?

Terraces.

CHAIRMAN: OK, here's the deal. We'll pay you £5,000 a week this year, then £10,000 a week next season.
PLAYER: Sounds good. I'll come back next season.

⚽ What do you say to a football player with cheese in his ears?

🏆 **Anything you like – he can't hear you!**

⚽ Which sport do good-looking footballers play?

🏆 **The beautiful game.**

⚽ What type of footballer is best at lighting a match?

🏆 **A striker.**

⚽ An injured player is sent to the club physiotherapist to discuss a new training regime, designed to help him recover as quickly as possible.
PHYSIO: Tell me, how flexible are you?
PLAYER: Well, I can't make Mondays or Thursdays.

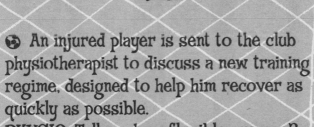

iN THE BOOK

EVER WONDERED WHAT
A FOOTBALLER HAS ON
HIS BOOKSHELF?

HOW TO SCORE BY EAMON TARGET

WHEN'S HALF-TIME? by Mustafa Pee

HAT TRICK! BY SHELLEY BRATE

BURST BALL BY D. FLATED

Over the Line? by Justin da Net

THE STRETCHER BY CARRIE MEHOFF

PENALTY? BY SHIRLEY KNOTT

Confessions of a Referee by I. C. Clearly

HOW TO STAY FIT BY X. HAUSTED

Aiming
for Goal
by
E. Shoots

IN THE BACK OF THE NET BY ANDY SCORES

How to Beat a Defender by C. U. Later

SiLLY STADiUMS

FOUR PAGES FULL TO CAPACITY WiTH SUPER-SiLLY STADiUM JOKES!

🌐 What do you call a girl who stands at the end of the pitch and catches the ball?

🏆 Annette.

⚽ What runs around a football pitch, but does not move?

🏆 A fence.

⚽ Why was the pitch waterlogged?

🏆 Players kept dribbling on it.

⚽ Why did the football pitch become a triangle?

🏆 Someone took a corner.

⚽ What's the angriest part of a goal?

🏆 The crossbar.

⚽ What is the hungriest part of the goal?

🏆 The goalmouth.

⚽ Why is it easy to predict the weather on match days?

🏆 There are always showers after the game.

⚽ What do football teams do if the pitch is flooded?

🏆 Bring on their subs.

⚽ Which is the chilliest ground in the Premiership?

🏆 Cold Trafford.

⚽ Which part of a football ground never stays the same?

🏆 The changing rooms.

⚽ Manager: Our next game is tricky. It's at our bogey ground - we never play well there.

🏆 Captain: Er, boss, it's at home.

⚽ When does a football pitch have more than four corners?

🏆 When it's a brilliant game!

FREAKY FANS

FOOTY FANS ARE A WEIRD BUNCH. BUT WE BET YOU NEVER KNEW JUST HOW WEIRD - UNTIL NOW!

⚽ As the crowd filed out after a boring 0–0 draw, the PA system announced: 'This is a message for Mr Taylor. Your wife has been taken to hospital as she has just gone into labour.'

'Poor bloke,' one fan said to his mate. 'He had to sit through that rubbish, now he's got to go home and make his own tea.'

⚽ CHARLTON FAN: Five minutes' stoppage time? Where did that come from?

BOLTON FAN: Don't you remember? The ref had to write Hermann Hreidarsson and Stylianos Giannakopoulos into his notebook.

A Scottish football fan goes into a sports shop to buy a shirt. 'Do you have the latest Scottish strip?' he asks.

'I'm sorry,' replies the assistant. 'We've sold out.'

'Oh. Can I have a wasp instead, please?' asks the fan.

'A wasp? What are you talking about? We don't sell wasps!' replies the assistant.

'Well, how come you've got one in the window?!'

Two football fans were stranded on a desert island.

'Our team lost today,' sighed the first

'How do you know?' asked the second.

'It's Saturday,' the first replied.

⚽ Did you hear about the crowd of potatoes who were watching a football match?

🏆 **They kept their eyes peeled.**

⚽ One fan to another (gloomily): Our team's so bad that Manager of the Month isn't an award. It's an appointment.

⚽ What do you call a microscopic football fan?

🏆 **A speck-tator.**

tiny footballer

⚽ FAN 1: Have you heard? We've just signed a new goal-keeper from Spain. He has a fish for a head and clothes pegs where his legs should be.

FAN 2: Where did we get him from?

FAN 1: Surreal Madrid.

⚽ What do very young football fans take to matches?

🏆 Rattles.

⚽ Why was the football stadium so chilly?

🏆 It was full of fans.

THE BEST
AND
THE REST

EVERY WORLD CUP HAS MOMENTS FANS REMEMBER BUT PLAYERS WANT TO FORGET! HERE ARE SOME DAFT PREDICTIONS ABOUT WHAT MIGHT HAPPEN IN GERMANY 2006 . . .

⚽ CRAFTIEST FREE KICK

England v Germany. David Beckham wins a free kick 25 yards from goal, but the Germans have lined up ten players in a defensive wall. In a moment of crafty genius, Beckham complains that his hairband has fallen out and asks if anyone can see it on the ground. When the helpful Germans bend down to help him look for it, Beckham lashes the ball over them into the net.

⚽ SNEAKIEST DEFENDING

Portugal v Argentina. During the first corner of the game, Argentinian defender Gabriel Heinze sneakily ties his shoelaces to those of speedy Portuguese winger Cristiano Ronaldo. No matter how fast he runs, for some reason Ronaldo just can't shake Heinze off!

⚽ MOST EMBARRASSING OWN GOAL

Brazil v Ukraine. Brazil's Roberto Carlos hits a free kick so hard it smacks off the crossbar, hits every player on the pitch and flies into his own goal at the other end. If only he was playing pinball!

BEST SAVE

England v Holland. The England keeper is down injured and Ruud van Nistelrooy is about to thump the ball into the top corner for Holland. Amazing the crowd with his quick thinking, Rio Ferdinand braids his hair into a mini net and catches the ball in it just in time!

😊 BEST HEADER

Argentina v Australia. Drawing 1-1 with a minute to go, Australia win one last corner. Australian striker Mark Viduka hasn't outjumped the Argentinian defence all game, but winger Harry Kewell has the brilliant idea to give him a piggyback.

Together they tower over the Argentinian keeper, and from the corner kick Viduka rockets the ball into the net off his head.

😊 WORST REFEREE

Spain v USA. Referee Ernesto Bauer starts the match with a brand-new red card, which he bought that morning, in his pocket. After just ten seconds he sends off the Spanish captain - just to see if it works!

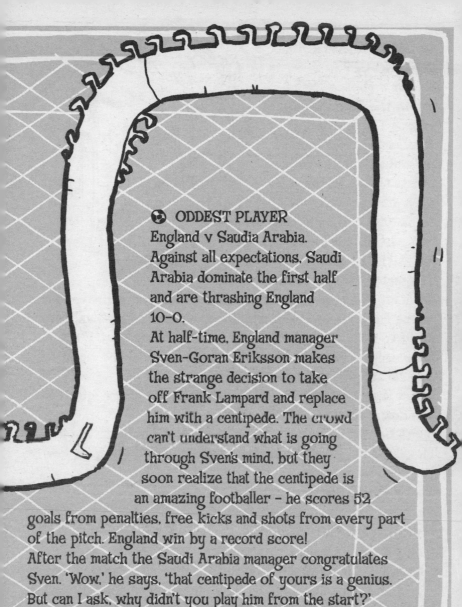

⚽ ODDEST PLAYER

England v Saudia Arabia.
Against all expectations, Saudi
Arabia dominate the first half
and are thrashing England
10–0.
At half-time, England manager
Sven-Goran Eriksson makes
the strange decision to take
off Frank Lampard and replace
him with a centipede. The crowd
can't understand what is going
through Sven's mind, but they
soon realize that the centipede is
an amazing footballer – he scores 52
goals from penalties, free kicks and shots from every part
of the pitch. England win by a record score!
After the match the Saudi Arabia manager congratulates
Sven. 'Wow,' he says, 'that centipede of yours is a genius.
But can I ask, why didn't you play him from the start?'
'Oh, I'd have liked to,' replies Sven, 'but it takes him
45 minutes to get his boots on!'

⚽ MOST DISASTROUS SENDING-OFF

France v Mexico. Everyone in the French team except Thierry Henry is suffering from food poisoning, but the referee insists the match must be played. Henry takes to the pitch to play Mexico by himself, while the rest of the team watch the game on TV at their hotel.

The match starts and the French team are soon celebrating from their sickbeds as Henry scores in the fifth minute. He is winning the game on his own! Too tired to watch, they have a nap and switch on the TV again later, only to see that Mexico have equalized in the eighty-ninth minute and the match has finished 1-1.

When Henry returns to the team hotel, he is distraught. 'I've let you down,' he sobs. 'I've let you all down.'

'Don't be stupid,' his teammates say to comfort him. 'You played Mexico all on your own and you only conceded one goal. How have you let us down?'

Henry sobs, 'I got sent off after 12 minutes.'

⚽ NASTIEST TACKLE

England v Germany II. In the World Cup Final, the capacity crowd watch as Wayne Rooney dribbles his way towards the goal. Just as he is about to shoot, three large defenders all hit him with a sliding tackle at the same time, and he goes down under a pile of thrashing arms and legs.

Regaining consciousness a few moments later, Wayne looks at the crowd and gasps, 'How did they all get back in their seats so quickly?'

WANTED!

On Thursday 24 October,
the trophy room
at Macclesfield Town FC
was broken into and
the contents stolen.

Police are looking for a man
with a carpet, two spiders
and some cobwebs.

If a member of the public sees this man,
on no account should he be approached.

Just point and laugh.

23

SUPERSTAR GAGS

THE HEROES OF THE BEAUTIFUL GAME ARE ALWAYS GOOD FOR A LAUGH.

⚽ Gary Neville was signing autographs after a big victory. He signed one for a young fan, who then promptly rejoined the queue of autograph hunters and waited until he got Gary's autograph again. Then he rejoined the queue and waited once more.

When he got to the front for the third time, Gary spoke to him. 'Now, look here, this is the third time you've asked for my autograph. What's going on?'

'Well,' said the young fan, 'if I can get ten more of yours, I can swap them for one of Rio Ferdinand's.'

⚽ Who is the cheekiest footballer?

🏆 Wayne Mooney.

⚽ BROOKLYN BECKHAM: Dad, can you do my English homework for me?
DAVID: Son, that wouldn't be right now, would it?
BROOKLYN: Probably not, but you could at least try.

⚽ Why should Roy Keane be kept 100 metres underground?

🏆 Because deep down he's a very nice person.

⚽ PUNDIT: Heskey went down very easily under that challenge.
COMMENTATOR: Yes, he did seem to make Emile of it.

⚽ 'Which footballers can help you cross a river?'
'I don't know.'
'Kanu, Wayne Bridge and the Neville brothers.'
'Why the Neville brothers?'
'Because they're a pair of planks!'

⚽ Darius Vassell walks up to a girl and says, 'Hello, love, can I have a kiss?'
'Ooh,' she says, 'you're a little forward.'

⚽ Did you hear that Ashley Cole and Cheryl Tweedy are releasing a song together?

🏆 They're calling themselves Goals Allowed.

⚽ How does West Brom's Japanese star travel to matches?

🏆 In a moto'.

⚽ Who is the moodiest player at Arsenal?

🏆 Sulk Campbell.

Are you better at football on the games console than you are in real life?

Well, now you can be the best player on the pitch without getting your legs all muddy, thanks to . . .

FRANKEN-BOOTS

. . . the new remote-controlled football boots from SONYBOK.

Simply place them on the feet of a friend or gullible younger brother, pick up the controller and, hey presto, your very own real-life remote-controlled player!

You can make him do dozens of realistic moves . . .

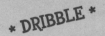
* DRIBBLE *

* SHOOT *

* PASS *

* TRIP OVER HIS SHOELACES *

* JUMP UP AND DOWN IN A TANTRUM *

* RUN INTO THE GIRLS' CHANGING ROOM FOR A DARE *

DON'T DELAY, BUY ONE TODAY!

Warning – SONYBOK cannot be held responsible if you lose a friend because you send him out to play in the pouring rain, while you sit in the car and stay dry.

NOT-SO-MASTERFUL MANAGERS

WHO PUT THIS LOT IN CHARGE?

⚽ Did you hear about the manager caught shaking a cat up and down in his office?

🏆 He was hoping to find some more money in the transfer kitty.

⚽ Who is the dullest manager in the league?

🏆 **David O'Dreary.**

⚽ The local football team were having a dreadful season. They hadn't won a game for months and the manager was at the end of his tether.

'Look,' suggested a friend one evening, 'why don't you take the whole squad out for a 10-mile run every day?'

'What good will that do?' moaned the manager.

'Well,' replied his friend, 'today's Sunday. By next Saturday they'll be 60 miles away and you won't have to worry about them!'

⚽ A Birmingham City player was talking to his friends. 'Our manager won't stand for any nonsense,' he said. 'Last Saturday he caught a couple of fans climbing over the wall and went bananas. He grabbed them by their collars and said, "Now you just get back in there and watch the game until it finishes!"'

MANAGER: I propose we ditch our hi-tech football boots and play in good old-fashioned gumboots.
CAPTAIN: Don't be crazy. We'll be wellygated!

INTERVIEWER: Any ideas about how you'll halt this dismal run of results?
MANAGER: Well, we're changing the name of the club to What a Load of Rubbish FC. At least then it will sound like the fans are getting behind us.

One player to another: Father Christmas was our manager once – but he got the sack in December.

⚽ A manager goes to his doctor to find out why he gets out of breath during training. 'Your problem is you're too fat,' says the doctor. 'I'd like a second opinion,' demands the manager. 'OK,' replies the doctor. 'You're ugly.'

⚽ Manager: Twenty teams in the league and you lot finish bottom.
Captain: It could have been worse.
Manager: How exactly?
Captain: There could have been more teams.

⚽ MANAGER: I confidently predict we'll stay in the Premiership for three seasons.
REPORTER: Yeah, autumn, winter and spring!

🌀 The manager of a club was talking to a young player who had applied for a trial. 'Do you kick with both feet?' asked the manager.

'Don't be silly!' said the trialist. 'If I kicked with both feet, I'd fall over!'

🌀 MANAGER: We have a very tough game coming up against Snottingham Forest.
REPORTER: Don't you mean Nottingham Forest?
MANAGER: No, Snottingham. They're our bogey team.

🌑 REPORTER: So, you've resigned. Weren't the crowd behind you?
MANAGER: They were behind me all right, but I managed to shake them off at the station.

🌑 MANAGER: Is your poor performance down to ignorance or apathy?
PLAYER: I don't know and I don't care.

🌑 Sir Alex Ferguson: Did you know you can buy footballers at IKEA?
Arsene Wenger: Sure, last week I bought a flat-pack four.

⚽ Why do managers take suitcases to away games?

🏆 So they can pack the defence.

⚽ What do Bolton players use to play Monopoly?

🏆 Sam Allar-dice.

NEWSFLASH!
Birmingham manager Steve Bruce is taking his players on a course to teach them about dog training. He's hoping it will teach them how to hold on to a lead.

⚽ What's the difference between God and José Mourinho?

🏆 God doesn't think he's José Mourinho.

NEWSFLASH!
Chelsea continue to spend ridiculous amounts of money. Only last week they spent millions to widen all the door frames at Stamford Bridge – to allow José Mourinho's head to fit through them.

CLEVER CLOGS

SO YOU THINK YOU KNOW THE RULES OF THE BEAUTIFUL GAME? TEST YOURSELF WITH SOME FIENDISHLY UGLY QUESTIONS. (ANSWERS ON P. 41.)

1. What must every player have in his socks?
a) His hands
b) His shinguards
c) His dinner money

2. What item of jewellery is a player allowed to wear during a match?
a) A necklace, as long as it spells 'Mum'
b) A watch, in case the referee's stops
c) None

3. Why must a substitute coming on to the pitch show the fourth official the bottom of his shoes?
a) To check his studs are the right length
b) To check he hasn't stepped in dog poo
c) To check he hasn't left the price label on

4. What happens if the ball bursts during the game?
a) The referee starts crying
b) The game is abandoned and replayed the following week
c) The match is restarted by dropping a new ball where the original one burst

5. What happens if the crossbar snaps?
a) The goalkeeper gets hit on the head
b) The game is abandoned unless the crossbar can be fixed
c) The goalposts are removed and replaced with jumpers

6. Can the referee send a player off after he has blown the final whistle?
a) No
b) Yes. The referee can send a player off until he leaves the field of play
c) Yes. The referee can send a player off any time until the player's next birthday

7. What happens if a team has fewer than seven players?
a) They get thrashed
b) The crowd laugh at them because they don't have enough friends
c) The referee will not allow the game to begin

8. Why does the fourth official hold up a board with a number on it near the end of the game?
a) He is announcing that week's winning lottery numbers
b) He is awarding the winning team marks out of ten
c) He is announcing how many minutes of extra time there are

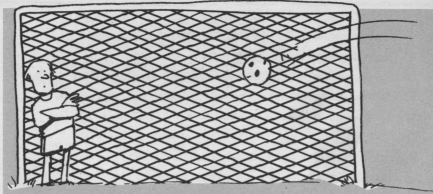

9. If the keeper has the ball in his hands, how long can he keep it before he kicks it out again?
a) Six seconds
b) Sixty seconds
c) If it's his ball, as long as he wants

10. What happens if a player takes off his shirt to celebrate a goal?
a) He catches a cold
b) He shows the referee his hairy chest
c) The referee shows him a yellow card

11. Who decides in which end of the ground a penalty shoot-out is taken?
a) The referee decides
b) The team that goes first in the shoot-out decides
c) Whichever end of the stadium shouts the loudest gets the shoot-out at their end

12. If the ball hits the referee and goes into the goal, what happens?
a) It's not a goal
b) It's a goal, but you won't see the referee celebrating
c) It's a goal and the referee is allowed to run around screaming, with his shirt over his head

ANSWERS

1.	b		7.	c
2.	c		8.	c
3.	a		9.	a
4.	c		10.	c
5.	b		11.	a
6.	b		12.	b

HOW DID YOU DO?

10-12: You are indeed a clever clogs. Be careful when you head the ball, you might damage that enormous brain of yours!

7-9: You know the rules of the game pretty well. Well enough to know when you're breaking them!

4-6: You need to brush up on your knowledge of football. It sounds like you turn up for matches carrying a snorkel and a cricket bat!

0-3: Are you a referee? You hardly know the rules at all!

ALL-TIME ANIMAL X1

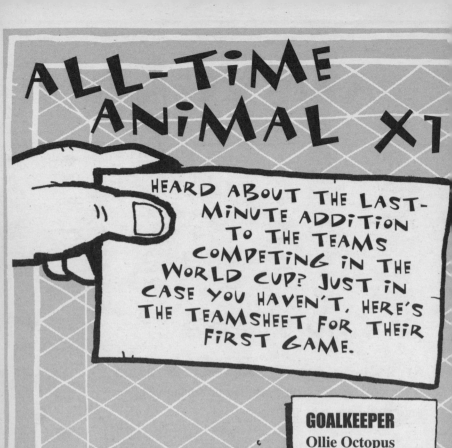

HEARD ABOUT THE LAST-MINUTE ADDITION TO THE TEAMS COMPETING IN THE WORLD CUP? JUST IN CASE YOU HAVEN'T, HERE'S THE TEAMSHEET FOR THEIR FIRST GAME.

GOALKEEPER
Ollie Octopus
✔ Eight arms for making saves
✘ Keeps getting caught in the net!

DEFENCE
Gomez Goat
✔ Confuses the opposition by eating the penalty spot
✘ Annoys his teammates by gobbling up all the half-time oranges

DEFENCE
Stevie Skunk
✔ So smelly he makes the opposition run the wrong way!
✘ Refuses to take a shower after the game

DEFENCE
Barney Boa Constrictor
✔ Good at marking – wraps himself around strikers and doesn't let go
✘ Has a nasty habit of squeezing the opposition until they burst

MIDFIELD
Billy Bull
✔ His charging runs scare the opposition to pieces (especially if they're wearing red)
✘ Always gets sent off in the first five minutes

DEFENCE
David Donkey
✔ The hardest kick in football
✘ Easily distracted by a juicy blade of grass

MIDFIELD
Harry Hamster
✔ Brilliant at dribbling – he runs on the inside of the ball!
✘ When his teammates are screaming for him to cross, he's often too busy having a sleep

MIDFIELD
Mohammed Mole
✔ Evades his marker by making his runs under the pitch
✘ Too short-sighted to see the ball!

MIDFIELD
Freddie Flea
✔ The fastest player on the pitch
✘ More interested in passing himself from player to player than passing the ball

STRIKER
Sammy Salmon
✔ Wins plenty of penalties by diving in the box
✘ Can only play on wet days

STRIKER
Jermaine Giraffe
✔ At 3 metres tall, excellent at heading the ball
✘ Too big to fit in the team bus!

MANAGER
Lennie Lion – if the players don't do what he says, he eats them!

ANIMAL FOOTBALL FAQ

ANSWERS TO ALL THOSE QUESTIONS ABOUT ANIMAL FOOTBALL YOU WERE AFRAID TO ASK!

⚽ What bounds across Australia, scoring great goals?

🏆 A kanga-rooney.

⚽ What did the ref say to the chicken who tripped a defender?

🏆 Fowl!

⚽ Do grasshoppers watch football?

🏆 **No, they prefer cricket.**

⚽ Why didn't the dog play football?

🏆 **Because it was a boxer.**

⚽ Why did a couple of young cows chase a ball around a football pitch?

🏆 **It was a game of two calves.**

⚽ Why did the bird flap along the side of the pitch?

🏆 **It was a winger.**

⚽ What did the
footballing bee say?

🏆 **Hive scored!**

⚽ Which insect
doesn't play well
in goal?

🏆 **The fumble
bee.**

⚽ Why are there no football matches in safari parks?

🏆 **There are too many cheetahs.**

⚽ What has
twenty-two legs and
swims in the sea?

🏆 **A football
squid.**

ELEPHANTS V ANTS

It was a boring Sunday afternoon in the jungle, so the Elephants decided to challenge the Ants to a game of football.

The game was going well, with the Elephants beating the Ants ten goals to nil, when the Ants gained possession. The Ants' star player was dribbling the ball towards the Elephants' goal when the Elephants' left back suddenly came lumbering towards him, trod on the little ant and killed him instantly.

The referee stopped the game. 'What do you think you're doing? Do you call that sportsmanship, killing another player?'

The elephant replied, 'I'm sorry, I didn't mean to – I was just trying to trip him up!'

New from Penault, it's the sports car that every footballer should own . . .

The
Penault-Y

With loads of features that every footballer will love . . .

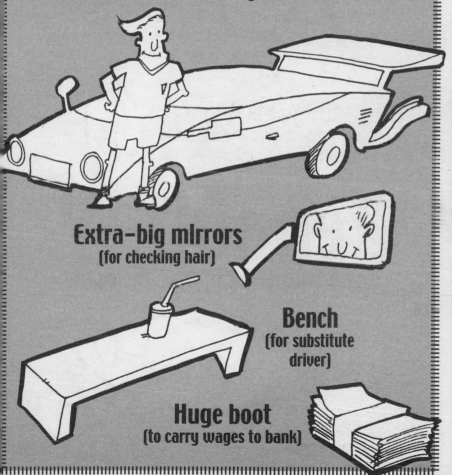

Extra-big mirrors
(for checking hair)

Bench
(for substitute driver)

Huge boot
(to carry wages to bank)

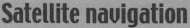

Satellite navigation
(for the player who has so many cars he needs help finding the way out of his garage)

Glove compartment
(handy for goalkeepers)

Extra-strong headlights
(can be used as floodlights if you want to have a kick-about on your front lawn)

The Penault-Y

Costs only £500,000 on the road.

Or £2.50 off the road.
Because if it's off the road,
it means you've crashed it.

GOALKEEPER BLUES

GOALKEEPING CAN BE A LONELY JOB. YOU CAN STAND THERE FOR A WHOLE MATCH AND HARDLY TOUCH THE BALL. WE ASKED SOME TOP GOALKEEPERS HOW THEY LIKE TO PASS THE TIME BETWEEN SAVES.

Danny Coyne (Burnley and Wales)

I amuse the crowd by putting my goalkeeping gloves over my ears and pretending I'm an elf.

Paul Robinson (Tottenham and England)

I like to climb the netting and pretend I'm a spider in a web, waiting for flies.

Craig Gordon (Hearts and Scotland)
I like to walk along the goal line and pretend it's a circus high wire that I could fall off any second!

Maik Taylor (Birmingham City and Northern Ireland)
I like to arm-wrestle with the crowd, four at a time.

David James (Manchester City and England)
I see how many blades of grass I can count before I accidentally count the same one twice. My record is 11,316. Or was it 11,315? Tsk. I'll have to start again now.

Robert Green (Norwich City and England)
I hide a mobile phone inside my glove and sneakily ring people on it. The manager thinks I'm clapping my hands to encourage the team, but actually I'm ordering pizza.

GORMLESS GOALIES

GOALKEEPERS AREN'T WELL KNOWN FOR THEIR SENSE OF HUMOUR. BUT THESE JOKES ARE SURE TO MAKE EVEN THEM CHUCKLE!

⚽ Why should you never put a vampire in goal?

🏆 Because they can't handle crosses.

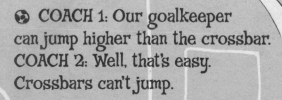

⚽ COACH 1: Our goalkeeper can jump higher than the crossbar.
COACH 2: Well, that's easy. Crossbars can't jump.

⚽ After a hard game, a goalkeeper walks into the treatment room.

'You've got to help me,' he says to the physiotherapist. 'I'm in agony all over.'

The physiotherapist is very concerned. 'Were you fouled?' he asks the goalkeeper.

'No,' the keeper replies.

'Did you fall awkwardly?' the physiotherapist asks.

'No,' the keeper replies.

The physiotherapist is baffled. 'Show me where it hurts,' he says.

So the keeper touches himself on the leg. 'OW! It hurts there.' Then he touches his earlobe. 'OW!! It hurts there too!' Then he touches his hair. 'OW!!!!! EVEN MY HAIR HURTS!'

The physiotherapist examines the keeper, then shakes his head. 'You fool,' he says to the keeper. 'You don't hurt all over. You've broken your finger!'

⚽ What did the crowd shout when the ghost flew into the back of the net?

🏆 Ghoul!

⚽ How does a keeper send his Christmas cards?

🏆 By goalpost.

⚽ Did you hear about the goalie with the heavy piggy bank?

🏆 He was always saving.

⚽ Paul Robinson was walking down
the street one day when he heard
shouts coming from the nearby museum.
He looked up to see smoke billowing from
a fourth-storey window, and a man leaning out holding
a vase.

'Help, help!' the man shouted. 'I need someone to catch
the museum's most important piece! It's the oldest
vase in the world and worth millions of pounds!'
A crowd of onlookers had gathered, but no one was
confident of catching a vase dropped from such a
great height. Until Robinson stepped forward.
'I'm the England goalkeeper,' he shouted to the man.
'I'm famous for my safe hands. Drop the vase. It'll be
like catching a ball.'
And with that he adopted the classic goalkeeper's
stance – legs apart and slightly bent at the knees,
arms stretched away from his body with palms facing
forward.
'OK!' shouted the man. 'I'll trust you. I've no choice!
Here it comes!'
So, with the flames roaring all around him, the man
threw the vase from the window. But just as he let go,
the vase clipped the edge of the window sill so that
it was sent spinning away from the goalkeeper as it
tumbled through the air.

The man in the museum shouted, 'What have I done?!' and the crowd gasped, all sure that the priceless vase would shatter on the pavement.

Robinson though remained still as the vase fell, spinning and tumbling further and further away from him. Then, when the vase was only centimetres from the ground, he dived a full 7 metres across the pavement, caught the vase in his outstretched right hand and pulled it safely into his chest. The crowd erupted into cheers. Robinson, still clutching the vase to his chest with his right arm, waved to the crowd of onlookers to acknowledge their appreciation. Then, without thinking, he turned away from them, held out the vase and kicked it 60 metres down the road. Oops!

EVEN MORE PREPOSTEROUS PLAYERS

DID YOU HEAR ABOUT THE STAR STRIKER WHO PERFORMED CIRCUS TRICKS? HE WAS ON THE BALL.

What happened to the football player who wore too much aftershave?

He was scent off.

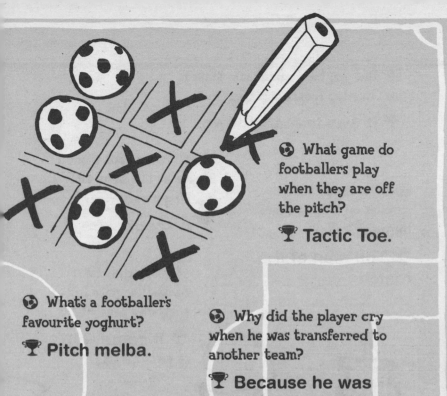

⚽ What game do footballers play when they are off the pitch?

🏆 Tactic Toe.

⚽ What's a footballer's favourite yoghurt?

🏆 Pitch melba.

⚽ Why did the player cry when he was transferred to another team?

🏆 Because he was moved.

⚽ Why did the football player stay on the pavement?

🏆 Because he was a rotten crosser.

⚽ What do footballers drink?

🏆 Penal-tea.

⚽ Did you hear about the time it was raining football players?

🏆 **It was teaming down.**

⚽ Who can spot a good player at the same time as lighting a campfire?

🏆 **A scout.**

⚽ Who lights the candles on a footballer's birthday cake?

🏆 **The man of the match.**

⚽ Why did the footballer hate his birthday present?

🏆 **It came with a red card.**

⚽ Did you hear about the footballer whose habits rubbed off on the other players?

🏆 **He was a transfer.**

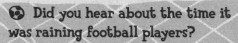

⚽ Why did the striker need antibacterial face wash?

🏆 Because of the penalty spot.

⚽ Why did the footballer bring the deep-fat fryer on to the pitch?

🏆 Because he'd chipped the ball.

⚽ Did you hear about the midfielder who kept all of the ballroom dancers really calm?

🏆 He had superb ball control.

⚽ Why did the footballer start jumping over a rope in the middle of the pitch?

🏆 He was the skipper.

ANATOMY OF A REFEREE

(Latin name: *Eejit maximus*)

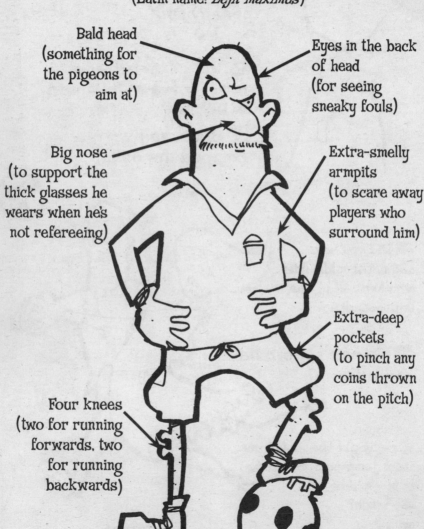

Bald head (something for the pigeons to aim at)

Eyes in the back of head (for seeing sneaky fouls)

Big nose (to support the thick glasses he wears when he's not refereeing)

Extra-smelly armpits (to scare away players who surround him)

Extra-deep pockets (to pinch any coins thrown on the pitch)

Four knees (two for running forwards, two for running backwards)

oi! REF!

JUST DON'T TRY TELLING ANY OF THESE JOKES TO A REFEREE WHEN YOU'RE ON THE PITCH – OR YOU MIGHT BE OFF IT SHORTLY AFTERWARDS!

⚽ The football club dance was in full swing when three strangers arrived and demanded admission. 'May I see your tickets, please?' said the club secretary.
'We haven't got any tickets,' said one of them. 'We're friends of the referee.'
'Get out of here!' said the club secretary. 'Whoever heard of a referee with three friends!'

What's the difference between a referee and a broken clock?

Even a broken clock is right twice a day!

Did you hear about the hippie referee?

He kept giving out mellow cards.

Pat: We're starting a football team. Would you like to join?
Matt: Sorry, I'm afraid I don't know the first thing about the game.
Pat: That's OK, we need a ref as well.

⚽ Ref: I'm sending you off.
Player: What for?
Ref: The rest of the match.

⚽ PLAYER: Could you send me off just for something I was thinking?
REF: No, of course I couldn't.
PLAYER: Good. Because I think you're an idiot.

⚽ What did the ref show the cowardy-custard footballer?

🏆 **The yellow card.**

⚽ If you have a referee in football, what do you have in bowls?

🏆 **Soup.**

Why did the ref snap his stopwatch in two?

It was half-time.

How do you know when a referee is enjoying his job?

He whistles while he works.

EVEN MORE SUPERSTAR GAGS

⚽ Wayne Rooney goes shopping and spots a Thermos flask. 'What's that for?' he asks.

'It's to keep hot things hot and cold things cold,' says the salesman.

Wayne thinks it's a brilliant idea and buys one to take home and show to his mum. 'It's to keep hot things hot and cold things cold,' he says.

'You ought to take it to work,' she tells him. So he takes it to training the following day.

'What've you got there, son?' asks Sir Alex Ferguson.

'It's to keep hot things hot and cold things cold,' says Wayne.

'That's a good idea,' says Sir Alex. 'What have you got in it?'

'Coffee,' says Wayne. 'And some ice cream.'

⚽ Steven Gerrard and Jamie Carragher were in a car park after the match, trying to unlock the door of Gerrard's sports car with a coat hanger. They tried and tried to get the door open, but the lock just wouldn't give. Carragher stopped for a moment to catch his breath. 'It's no use,' he said. 'We're never going to get in.'
'We have to,' urged Gerrard. 'It's starting to rain and the top is down.'

NEWSFLASH!
Scientists are baffled by Manchester City goalie David James. They have been using him as a guinea pig in medical experiments. But, despite exposing him to several highly contagious diseases, extensive tests have shown that he can't catch anything.

⚽ Bob: The best club side of all time has to be
Manchester United's treble-winning side.
Jim: You're joking, aren't you? They were rubbish.
Bob: How can you say that? What about Ryan Giggs?
His mazy runs left defenders tied in knots.
Jim: Pah! Giggs, Schmiggs!
Bob: Well, what about David Beckham? His pinpoint
crosses provided countless goals for the forwards.
Jim: Pah! Beckham, Schmeckham!
Bob: Well, what about Roy Keane? Captain Courageous
led his men superbly and his tackling was frightening.
Jim: Pah! Keane, Schmeane!
Bob: Well, what about Peter Schmeichel . . .?

⚽ What do defender Olof Mellberg and
a turnip have in common?

🏆 They're both big Swedes.

⚽ What do Peter Crouch and a jigsaw have in common?

🏆 They both fall to pieces in the box.

⚽ RUUD: Sorry, boss. There's no way I can play unless I get a cortisone injection.
RIO: Hey, if he's getting a new car then I want one as well.

⚽ Ferguson: What's the matter? You seem distracted.

Rio Ferdinand: Sorry, boss. It's just that my sister's expecting a baby and I don't know whether I'm going to be an aunt or an uncle.

⚽ What do Michael Schumacher and David Beckham have in common?

🏆 **They both take corners at frightening speeds.**

⚽ What do you get if you cross Roy Keane and Danny Mills?

🏆 **Fouled, generally.**

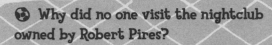 Why did no one visit the nightclub owned by Robert Pires?

🏆 It was a dive.

⚽ How does Ameobi score goals for Newcastle?

🏆 With Shola power.

⚽ Which footballer can't be tamed?

🏆 Robbie Savage.

GiVE THE REF A HAND

EVER WONDERED WHAT THE REFEREE AND ASSISTANT REFEREE'S SIGNALS MEAN? HERE'S A HANDY GUIDE . . .

Penalty!

Streaker!

Stop the match – half-time!

Stop the match – I need the toilet!

You're getting a red card!

You're getting a birthday card!

THE PREMIER LEAGUE OF FOOTBALL LEAGUE JOKES

PREMIER LEAGUE

1. In which league do sliced and fried potatoes play?
The Premierchip.

2. What do Rangers and a three-pin
plug have in common?
They're both useless in Europe.

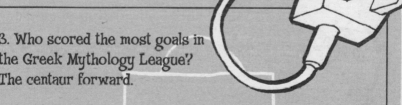

3. Who scored the most goals in
the Greek Mythology League?
The centaur forward.

4. Which team is never introduced to each other before
kick-off?
Queens Park Strangers.

PREMIER LEAGUE

5. Why don't Norwich City make as much money from selling players as they would like?
Because Canaries go cheap.

6. What do you hear when a Sheffield Wednesday player tells a joke in the dressing room?
Owls of laughter.

7. Network Rail are to be the new sponsors of West Bromwich Albion. They said they had a lot in common because both suffer regular points failures.

8. Sunderland have announced a sponsorship deal with Wrigley's chewing gum. You can always find them stuck to the bottom of a table.

9. Why is there always a tense atmosphere at Pride Park?
Because every week there's a Derby match.

PREMIER LEAGUE

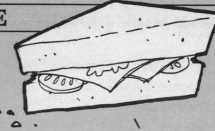

10. What's claret and blue
and delicious?
A West Ham sandwich.

11. What is the bluest sea in the world?
The Chelsea.

12. Chelsea owner Roman Abramovich is so
rich he doesn't change light bulbs, he just buys
a new mansion.

13. Which team do most Cub Scouts
support?
Knots County.

14. What do small
teams of Scottish
footballers play?
Fife-a-side.

15. Why doesn't Paul Jewell like
people touching his head?
Because he's got a Wigan.

PREMIER LEAGUE

16. What's Alan Shearer's favourite computer game?
Toon Raider.

17. What do West Ham players sing at Christmas?
Roy Carrolls.

18. Fire swept through a library at Old Trafford last night destroying thousands of books. A fire brigade spokesman said the real tragedy was that many of them had not even been coloured in yet.

PREMIER LEAGUE

19. What happened when the footballer ran out of salt and pepper in May?
It was the end of the seasoning.

20. Dad: What on earth are you doing?
Johnny: I've lined up all these vases and I'm kicking a football at them.
Dad: Why would you do that?
Johnny: I'm trying to hit them to improve my shooting accuracy. One day I want to play up front for the best team in north Wales.
Dad: Wrexham?
Johnny: Yeah, smashes 'em to bits, Dad.

A BIT OF A MUDDLE

DID YOU KNOW YOU CAN REARRANGE THE LETTERS OF FAMOUS AC MILAN DEFENDER PAOLO MALDINI TO SPELL I'M A LOO PAN LID?

Here are some more funny anagrams made by rearranging the letters in your favourite player's names . . .

Dennis Bergkamp
Pink German beds

Michael Owen
I chew a lemon

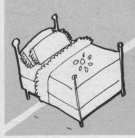

David Beckham
Mad hived back

Frank Lampard
Park farmland

Robbie Fowler
Fire lower, Bob!

Shaun Wright-Phillips
Hit whiplash slurping

AND HERE ARE THE NAMES OF SIX BRITISH CLUBS. CAN YOU UNTANGLE THEM TO WORK OUT THE NAME OF EACH CLUB?
(ANSWERS AT THE BOTTOM OF THE PAGE.)

1. Electric yetis
2. Synthetic cream
3. Spit hit tackler
4. Hip twin cows
5. Hunt nice red teams
6. Her sister married drink

IT'S A FUNNY OLD GAME . . .

THE MOST WEIRD, WONDERFUL AND JUST PLAIN BIZARRE FOOTY JOKES AROUND.

⚽ An amateur team Bowchester Athletic play their games at a ground several miles out of town, right next to a farm. During a match one Saturday afternoon, the ball was kicked clear out of the ground and landed in the farmyard, in the middle of a group of chickens and a rooster.

The rooster circled the ball for a few moments, studying it with interest. Then he turned to the chickens and announced, 'Ladies, I don't want to criticize, but I feel I must speak up. If this is the size of egg being turned out on the farm next door, you're just not trying hard enough.'

⚽ A school football match was taking place in the depths of winter. It had been raining heavily all week and the ground looked like a swamp.

However, the PE teacher ruled that play was possible and tossed the coin to determine ends.

The home captain won the toss and, after a moment's thought, said, 'OK – we'll take the shallow end.'

⚽ Why couldn't the car play football?

🏆 Because it only had one boot.

⚽ 'Dad, Dad!' cried Sam, as he arrived home one evening. 'I think I've been picked for the school football team.'
'That's great,' said his father. 'But why do you only think you've been picked? Aren't you sure? What position are you playing?'
'Well,' replied Sam, 'the team hasn't been announced yet, but I overheard the coach say I'd be the main drawback.'

⚽ Where do ex-footballers go if they want to become film stars?

🏆 **Volleywood.**

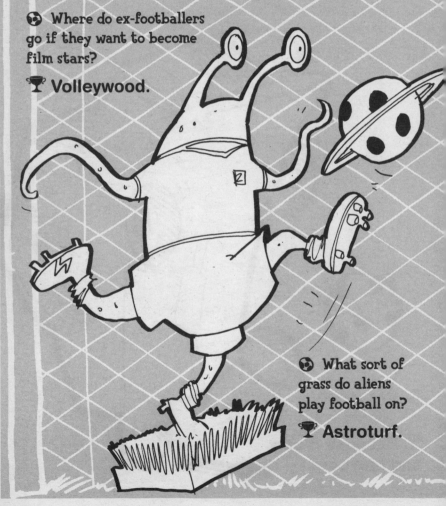

⚽ **What sort of grass do aliens play football on?**

🏆 **Astroturf.**

⚽ Ben knocked on the door of his friend's house. When his friend's mother answered he said, 'Can Tyler come out to play?'
'I'm sorry, no,' said his mother. 'He has a cold.'
'Well, then,' said Ben, 'can his football come out to play?'

⚽ TEAM NEWS
Star striker Tony Little is out of the Subbuteo Cup Final after sustaining a freak injury in training. Next door's Alsatian ran in and trod on his head.

⚽ Why does the team of artists never win?
🏆 They like to draw.

⚽ Did you hear about the soccer match between the characters from *Lord of the Rings*?
🏆 It was fantasy football.

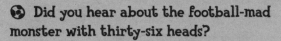

⚽ Did you hear about the football-mad monster with thirty-six heads?

🏆 **He had thirty-six caps.**

⚽ Johnny: What time are you playing football, Grandad?
Grandad: Football? At my age? What makes you ask that?
Johnny: Dad just said that when you kick off, we can all go to Disneyland.

⚽ Why was Cinderella bad at football?

🏆 **Because she ran away from the ball.**

😊 What did
the millionaire
caveman own?

🏆 His own club.

😊 What did they call
Dracula when his team
won the World Cup?

🏆 The champire

😊 What happened when
the teenager had a trial
with his local team?

🏆 He passed.

⚽ What do you get if you cross martial arts with soccer?

🏆 Kung Fu-tball.

⚽ Of all the things in a footballer's geometry set, which is the most complicated to describe?

🏆 The offside rule.

⚽ Did you hear about the monk who wanted to be a footballer?

🏆 He was trying to kick the habit.

😊 Why are football directors' meetings always so dull?

🏆 **They're held in the bored room.**

😊 PE teacher: William Webb Ellis invented rugby when, during a school football match, he picked up the ball and ran with it.
Student: Funny, when I did that last week, sir, you sent me off for deliberate handball and told me to go and see the headteacher.

😊 Whose job is it to carry the players to each game?

🏆 **The coach.**

😊 Did you hear about the magician who scored three goals while balancing a Stetson on his head?

🏆 **It was a hat trick.**

THE FINAL WHISTLE

⚽ Ronaldo, Thierry Henry and David Beckham find themselves standing before St Peter at the gates of Heaven. St Peter says to them, 'Before I open the gates, I will ask what you have done to deserve to enter the Kingdom of Heaven.' Ronaldo bows his head and says, 'I was the most famous player in the world, but I was born in the slums of Brazil with nothing. All my life I tried to show my fellow man what he could do if he worked hard and had faith.'

St Peter smiles, opens the gate and lets Ronaldo into Heaven. He turns to Thierry Henry and asks, 'What have you done to be allowed into Heaven?'

Henry bows his head and replies, 'I believe football is the food of life. Nothing else brings so much joy to so many people. I spent my life trying to entertain them and make them happy, even when I was not feeling happy myself.'

St Peter, moved by Henry's speech, opens the gates and lets him through too.

Finally, St Peter turns to David Beckham and says, 'And you, David, why are you here?'

David Beckham bows his head and says, 'Please, mister. Can I have my ball back?'